For
Atunkadmun

Kabbalah:
The Way of Light

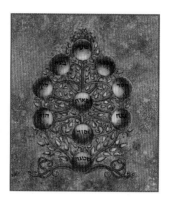

By Rabbi Lawrence Kushner

Illustrated by Jo Gershman

PETER PAUPER PRESS, INC.
WHITE PLAINS, NEW YORK

Designed by Arlene Greco

Text copyright © 1999
Rabbi Lawrence Kushner

Illustrations copyright © 1999
Jo Gershman

Published by Peter Pauper Press, Inc.
202 Mamaroneck Avenue
White Plains, NY 10601
All rights reserved
ISBN 0-88088-101-1
Printed in China
7 6 5 4 3 2 1

Contents

Introduction

Kabbalah begins with what you can see; it takes you to what you cannot. It is Judaism's mystical tradition. Like varieties of mysticism the world over, Kabbalah is Judaism's way of comprehending *and* experiencing the unity that lies just beneath the apparent brokenness, contradiction, and

confusion of everyday reality. In
the following pages, we shall
consider some of the ways the
Kabbalah envisions a mystical
approach to Judaism and life.
We begin with waking up.

Awakening—
More to Reality

The Baal Shem Tov, the father of Hasidism, the most recent revival of the Kabbalah, used to tell the following story:

Once there was a king who yearned for his subjects to be close to him. Being a wise ruler however, the king knew that if the process of getting close to him was too easy, people wouldn't think it was important. They would be convinced that something as awesome as being close to the king must be challenging and very difficult. So this is what

the king did. Since he was a magi-
cian, he built around himself a mag-
nificent castle with towers and gates
and walls. But it was all an illusion.
Then he issued a royal proclamation
inviting everyone to come and be
close to him. But when they arrived
and saw the fortress with all its bat-
tlements and walls, one by one they
all gave up. Surely such a task was
beyond human skill. But then the
child of the king came forward. She
was daunted but not dismayed.
Cautiously, deliberately, she went up
to the wall and extended her hand
to touch it, but as soon as she did,
the wall disappeared. And so it went
with all of the walls and towers and

gates. Illusions, every one of them!
In this way, she was able to walk
right up to her father who we imagine was simply sitting on a chair in
the middle of an open field. They
embraced, and he said, "What took
you so long?"

And just that is <u>the first prem-
ise of Kabbalah: There is more to
reality than meets the eye.</u> Let us

take a more contemporary meta-
phor. You are watching television.
Then you turn the sound all the way
down—as you used to do when you
were a kid during the commer-
cials—and laugh at the funny lady
whose lips moved without making
any sounds. Then you turn the con-
trast knob so that the speaker seems
barely visible through some dark
mist. Then you turn the brightness
all the way down so that the screen
is completely black. Now you see
nothing. You hear nothing. But you
continue staring at the black and
soundless glass television screen
because something is there. Someone is speaking. It's just that you

can't see or hear her. From within a darkened space a message issues.

Sefirot—
Inner Dynamic

Not only is there more to reality
than is apparent to our senses, but
the hidden infrastructure of being can
be known and understood. According
to the Kabbalah, this concealed
dimension of creation has ten
elements that exist in continuous
dynamic interrelationship.

These elements are like the
members of any extended family,
some of whom might not be in physi-
cal contact for long periods of time,
but who nevertheless influence one
another. Indeed, many family thera-
pists refuse to treat individuals but

instead insist on having the entire
family present for each session. We all
are who we are because of our rela-
tionships to others—and the more
primary the relationship, the more
powerful the influence.

Consider the simple situation,
for instance, in which a child gets
married. This obviously redirects
much of the emotional energy away
from the child's parents, just as the
child's new spouse becomes a new
player in the original family. The parents must now cope with a whole
slew of new emotions that gradually
affect their relationship to each other.
And this, in turn, influences how
they behave toward their other

children, who will also change how they respond to one another.

Just as someone might diagram the flow of emotional energy in a family system, so the Kabbalists seek to comprehend the infrastructure of creation and understand how each of its dimensions (or, in our imagery, "family members") affects the others. Each element is called a sefira (often confused with "sphere," because of their similar pronunciation). All ten, when diagrammed together, are referred to as the "sefirotic tree," the Faces of the King, or the World of Union. To understand how the sefirot affect one another is to understand how the world works. They can also

be understood therefore as the dimensions of inner psychic space or the dynamics of a personality as well. The sefirot are present everywhere, all the time. If they were in perfect balance, our world would be, too. But, alas, the world is a mess and our task, through holy deeds and religious devotion, is to restore the balance.

The highest sefira, the one closest to God, is called Keter (crown) or Ayn Sof (without end). Then come two modes of knowing, Hokhma (insight) and Bina (intuition). Below them are the two sides of parenting, Gevura (stern justice) and Hesed (unconditional love). Then comes Tiferet (harmony or beauty). Netsach (endurance) and

Hod (majesty), dimensions of power, come next. Supporting all of the above is Yesod (foundation). And finally, at the bottom, joining the whole constellation to everyday reality, is Shekhina (God's indwelling presence in our world). Often the sefirotic diagram portrays many of the sefirot on two sides, male and female, and places Tiferet (harmony) in the center, balancing everything. Sometimes the sefirot are also envisioned as a human archetype, the top three being the head, the next two the arms, and so on.

Torah—
Mystical Revelation

The word Kabbalah in Hebrew means the Jewish mystical tradition. It is a way of understanding and practicing Judaism. And, like everything in classical Judaism, Kabbalah also begins with studying God's revelation at Mount Sinai as recorded in the Five Books of Moses or the Torah.

According to the Zohar, Moshe de Leon's great 13th century master text of the Kabbalah, (which itself claims to be a commentary on the Torah!), scripture is like a beautiful princess hidden away in a tower. She has one secret lover. Out of his love

for her, the lover passes by her window each day hoping for a glimpse. She, in turn, opens the curtain, just enough to let him see her face, then quickly closes it again. No one else sees except the lover, but he understands that the intention of this fleeting vision is to awaken his love. It is the same way with studying the words of the Torah, says the Zohar. We study them daily hoping for a glimpse, an affirmation of requited love.

And so it goes, year after year, the lover and the hidden princess—or the student and the Torah—gradually becoming more intimate. First there are hints, then allusions and parables, until at last she reveals herself to him face to face and he is able to read and

understand all her secrets, hidden with her since before the creation of the world. In this way he becomes a complete person. She says to her lover, "Do you remember that word with which I first caught your attention? Now you understand the layers of hidden meaning beneath it. Now you understand why nothing should be added to or removed from the original text of the story. Everything in the biblical text is precisely the way it is supposed to be. Not even a single letter should be changed!"

In this way, each word in sacred scripture is given new mystical meaning. And each word is joined to every other word in new constellations of meaning. According to one

Kabbalistic tradition, when the
Messiah comes, the Messiah will
teach us how to pronounce the entire
Torah as one long, uninterruptible
Name of God. According to another
legend in the name of Rabbi Mendl
Torum of Rymanov, God did not give
the entire Torah on Sinai, nor did
God give the Ten Commandments,
nor did God give just the first utterance, "I am the Lord, your God,"
nor did God even give the first word
of the first utterance, "anokhi, I."
All God gave at Sinai was the first
letter of the first word which is the
first letter of the Hebrew alphabet:
aleph. But the aleph does not, as is
commonly misunderstood, have no
sound. The aleph is the sound the

larynx makes as it clicks into gear and might therefore be thought of as the mother of all articulate speech. It is the softest, yet still audible, sound there can be. And, according to still another legend in the Zohar, the entire Torah was contained in that first aleph. In the barely audible sound of almost breathing can be found the seed of God's entire revelation.

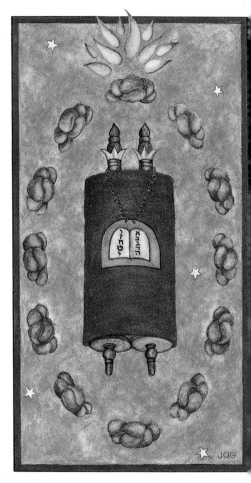

Mitzvot—
Sacred Deeds

*T*he study of Torah leads to action. Each religious deed (mitzvah) not only fulfills a divine commandment, it also contributes to restoring the inner balance of creation. In this way, each deed becomes a potential act of tikkun, or repair. According to one kabbalistic maxim, "Awakening here below causes an awakening on High." And for this reason, every human deed has literally cosmic significance.

According to one tradition, there are 613 commandments—365 positive and 248 prohibitions. Each commandment has its root in a different limb or organ of the human body.

When we behave in accordance with God's commandments we experience an actual physiological harmony with the world because we are acting in accord with it. The story is told in chapter 18 of Genesis of how Abraham ran to welcome wayfarers, thereby fulfilling one of the commandments. But how could this be? asks the Kabbalah. The Torah, the revelation of the commandments at Mount Sinai, had not yet been given! The answer is that since each holy deed has its source in the human anatomy, Abraham simply felt his feet walking toward the strangers and his mouth inviting them to stay in his home. The commandments only put into words what was already written into the structures of the human body and, indeed, all creation. To perform

a holy deed is to act in harmony with creation. Even more, it is to realign this world with the way God originally intended it to be. In this way, someone who lives in accord with the mitzvot (commandments) is attuned to the rhythm of being.

The story is told of how once, in the town of Safed, the richest man in town was sleeping, as usual, through worship. Every now and then, he would almost wake up, trying to get comfortable on the hard wooden bench, and then sink back into a deep sleep. One morning he awoke just long enough to hear the chanting of the Torah verses from Leviticus 24:5-6 in which God instructs the children of Israel to place twelve loaves of challah on a table in the

ancient wilderness tabernacle.

When services ended, the wealthy man woke up, convinced that God had come to him in a dream and asked him personally to bring twelve loaves of challah. The rich man felt a little foolish but went home and baked the bread. Upon returning to the synagogue, he decided the only proper place for his holy gift was with the Torah scrolls in the ark. So, he carefully arranged the loaves and said, "Thank You God for telling me what You want." Then he left.

No sooner had he gone than the poorest Jew in town, who was also the janitor, entered the sanctuary. All alone, he poured out his heart to God. "O Lord, I am so poor. My family is

starving. Unless You perform a miracle, we will surely perish." Then, as was his custom, he walked around the room to tidy it up. But when he opened the ark, there before him were twelve loaves of challah! "It's a miracle!" exclaimed the poor man. "I had no idea You worked like that! Blessed are You, O God, who answers our prayers." Then he ran home to share the bread with his family.

Minutes after he left, the rich man returned to the sanctuary—curious to know whether or not God really ate challah. Slowly he opened the ark. The challahs were gone! "Oh, my God!" he exclaimed, "You really ate the bread! I thought You were kidding. This is incredible. You can bet that next week there will be

another twelve loaves!"

So, the following week, the rich man brought another dozen loaves to the synagogue and again left them in the ark. And minutes later, the poor man entered the sanctuary. "God, I don't know how to say this, but I'm out of food again. Nothing is left. Unless You do another miracle, we surely will starve." He approached the ark and slowly opened its doors. "Another miracle!" he cried. "Twelve more loaves! Thank You God; this is wonderful!"

And so this exchanging loaves of bread became a regular weekly ritual, unnoticed by anyone else. It went on for twenty years! Then, one day, the rabbi observed this amazing sight: Rich man throws a dozen loaves of

challah into the ark and says, "Here, God, I'm in a hurry," and leaves, whereupon poor man runs in, grabs bread, says, "Thanks, God," and leaves.

The rabbi called the two men back together and told them what he had seen and what they had been doing. Now they realized that God didn't eat challah and God hadn't baked it either. And they feared that now God would no longer be present in their ritual. But then the rabbi said, "Now that you know God doesn't eat challah or bake challah, you will have to do something even more difficult. You will have to go on baking and eating the challah anyway. Look at your hands. They are the hands of God."

Adam Kadmon—
The Human Archetype

There were two Adams. The first was the one of the Garden of Eden—but according to the Kabbalah, there was also a second. This Adam (Adam Kadmon) was not so much an actual person but a golem, a primordial, archetypal human form that was an intermediary between God and all creation. Within him/her were the seeds of every subsequent generation.

Not only, therefore, is each human being built on the model of this primordial Adam but, according to Kabbalistic legend, each one of us

is descended from a part of that Adam. When we meet a stranger for whom we feel an immediate kinship, it may be that once our souls resided next to each other. But now, after our expulsion from Eden, we have been scattered like sparks throughout the universe yearning to return to our original home.

In the same way, we are each also miniature Adams and Eves, carrying within ourselves the DNA blueprint for humankind. According to the Midrash, Rabbi Simeon ben Rakish said in the name of Rabbi Eleazar ben Azriah: At the time the Holy One was creating Adam (the one in the garden), God came to the stage in creating him when Adam had the form of

an unshaped lump of clay, an unarticulated embryo, which lay prone from one end of the world to the other. Then the Holy One caused to pass before this golem each generation with its righteous men and women, each generation with its wicked men and women, each with its scholars, each with its leaders.

And this archetypal being is recreated in each embryo, which is likewise permitted to see from one end of creation to the other. And just as each human being is a microcosm of that primordial Adam, so too are we permitted fleeting glances of eternity.

Messengers of the Most High

*I*f everything is connected to every-thing else and each deed has poten-tially cosmic significance, then human beings are also instruments of the Most High. Sometimes they know it, sometimes they don't.

Near the end of the book of Genesis, Jacob sends Joseph to see how things are going with his brothers who are tending the family flocks in Shechem. It is essential to the plot line of the larger story that Joseph find them so that they can sell him into slavery in Egypt. Only this will initiate

Joseph's astonishing rise to power and the ultimate migration of the Jewish people down to Goshen. After all, if Joseph and his brothers do not go to Egypt, there can be no Passover, no exodus, no Mount Sinai, nothing.

It is critical, in other words, that Joseph find his brothers and his destiny. But when he gets to the fields of Shechem, they're not there! At pre-

cisely that moment, however, the text says, a man found Joseph wandering in the field and asked him what he was looking for. When Joseph told him, the man replied that he had overheard the brothers say they were going to Dothan. Joseph thanks him and sets out for Dothan, slavery, and ultimately the throne of Egypt. Yet if it had not been for that wanderer in the fields of Shechem, none of it would have happened. The man, without whom nothing would be the way it now is, does not even have a name! Surely he is a messenger of the Most High.

Imagine that your life is a one-thousand-piece, interlocking, jigsaw

puzzle set. The goal is to fit all the pieces together and, hopefully, die at a ripe old age. Now to make things interesting, no one seems to be issued a complete puzzle. Every one is missing, on average, about seven pieces and these, in turn, are randomly distributed into other people's puzzles. And so we spend our lives walking around asking one another things like, "Do you need a piece that's kind of bluish with a little yellow line in the corner?" And, sooner or later someone says, "My God, I've been looking for that piece my whole life!" "Here," we reply, "I don't know what to do with it. Take it, it's yours!" And in this way we are implicated in one

another's lives. Sometimes we don't even realize that we have given or received a puzzle piece from someone else until years and decades later—sometimes never. No matter, the errand has been completed.

Evil and
the Other Side

In most religious systems, evil is an independent force, in business for itself; in much of the Kabbalah, however, evil is only another, albeit distant, manifestation of God. This is not to say it's not evil, nor the source of great pain and grief. But, if God is the source of all creation, then, in order for any thing to have reality, it must also be an expression of the divine.

According to the Zohar, evil only has power when people forget that it is not a manifestation of God! The following parable is told:

There once was a king who
wanted to test his son to see if he
would be a worthy heir to the king-
dom. He had warned his son to stay
away from loose women. But then, as
a test, the king hired a woman and
instructed her to use all her wiles to
seduce the prince. The Zohar then
asks: But isn't the woman also just
another loyal servant of the king? If
the prince knew this there obviously
would be no test. Indeed, once he
realizes the woman is only working for
his father, her power over him evapo-
rates. It is the same with evil in the
universe. As long as we bifurcate our
world and our consciousness into
good guys and bad guys, the bad guys
have extraordinary power. But once

we realize that even the bad guys are working for God, we are able to find sparks of holiness in them and their power is radically diminished.

The Hasidim speak in a similar vein in what they call the doctrine of alien thoughts during prayer. According to this teaching, when you are in prayerful contemplation or worship and everything seems to be on the highest spiritual level, then, at that instant, you will be assailed by the most lascivious thought you've had in months. Your first reaction will be to say to the thought, "Not here! Can't you see what I'm trying to do? Come back later." But, of course, the harder you push the thought away,

the stronger it comes back. The reason for its resilience is neither your weakness nor its power, but rather your failure to recognize that the thought is not some alien thing but a part of your own psyche. Indeed, it has chosen precisely this moment of spiritual light to come out from the cellar of your unconsciousness. Like some deformed creature of your own creation, it sidles up to you and coaxes, "Please, master, may I pray with you?" So, instead of attempting to banish it, you should find something holy even in it and invite it to pray with you. For as soon as you do, its power over you will vanish; it will become your ally.

Just as you are the source of all your thoughts, even the evil ones, and just as realizing this will redeem these thoughts, so too it is with God and the apparent evil in creation. None of this is to suggest that evil is not ever present and dangerous. It is to say, however, that once we realize that God is indeed the creator of everything, we can endure and even prevail over much of the evil that assaults us daily from within ourselves and from without.

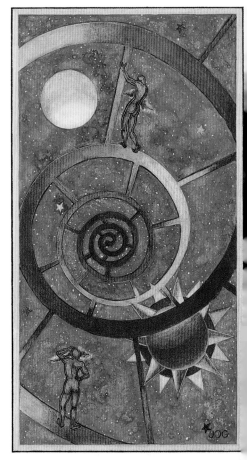

Yihud—
All Connected

*I*f everything is connected to everything else, then everything, even apparently trivial and painful things, must also have meaning. This doesn't necessarily mean that we can understand all these things or that we have to like them. But they are all manifestations of the hidden unity beneath and within all creation.

A story in the name of the Baal Shem Tov offers a novel interpretation of Psalm 37:23: "The steps of a person are ordered of the Lord, and He delights in his way." The Baal

Shem says it means that people journey to distant lands on business all the while convinced that they know where they are going and why. But God's thoughts are not like theirs. They think they are traveling far away merely to increase their wealth while God has other plans.

Thus, a person might eat a piece of bread in a far off country, thinking it is only part of a meal, when indeed he must eat precisely that piece of bread in that particular place. But the Lord has ordered the man's steps to make him wander far away in order to bring perfection to his soul. It might even happen, the Baal Shem continues, that the bread does not even concern the traveler himself, but rather one of his servants. Sometimes the

piece of bread is for the servant, but he is unable to undertake such an expensive journey. Then the master of the servant is influenced to make the journey for the sake of his servant, thereby enabling the servant to eat that bread ordained for him.

Alas, concludes the Baal Shem Tov, we do not usually understand any of this. On the contrary, we are aware only of a need to make a business trip, while our hearts are oblivious that it is all from God. We must remember therefore that we are not always going where we go for the reasons we imagine. Occasionally we are given a glimpse of what else is "coming down," but more than often than not we remain unaware.

Awareness—First Light

M ost people remember that "light" was the first thing God made in the creation sequence, as recorded in the opening chapter of Genesis. "And God said, 'Let there be light.' And there was light." Only a few people know on which day of the creation God created the sun, moon, stars and heavenly luminaries. The answer is the fourth day. You don't have to be a scholar to see that we have a problem here. If all the sources of light weren't made until day four, then from where did the light of day one come?

The Kabbalists solve the problem with a dazzling insight into the nature of consciousness. They explain that the light God made on the first day was not optical light, but the light of ultimate awareness or human consciousness raising itself from the dark oblivion of unconsciousness. It was a consciousness-like light so dazzling that, in it, Adam and Eve could gaze from one end of space to the other end of time. But then, when God saw that they couldn't be trusted to follow even one simple commandment ("Don't eat from the tree . . . "), God realized that they might take this light of ultimate awareness and destroy creation. But this only posed another problem. Were God to completely

withdraw that light of the first day,
the universe likewise could not
endure; it would implode. Therefore,
God took the light and hid it in the
material stuff of this world. There are
sparks of it in literally everything. In
the words of the psalmist, "Light is
hidden away for the righteous." And
whenever we behave in a holy way, we
"free" sparks and heighten our own
mystical awareness.

Ayn Sof— The Ocean

*T*he ultimate expression of the Kabbalist's union with God is called entering the ayin, the ultimate no-thingness. This is not, as it might first sound, nihilistic or even negative. The Kabbalists understand that any thing you could say about God would necessarily mean that there were other things also. But then God would cease to be infinite, boundless, all. They therefore often refer to God as Ayn Sof, meaning without end, infinite or, literally Nothing. And human beings, who through service and devotion experience that ultimate

Ayn Sof, likewise for a moment also become nothing.

Rabbi Michel of Zlotchov, a Hasidic master, explained it this way: People seek to be joined to God with all their hearts. They try to loose themselves from God and consider themselves to be nothing. This is because they understand that, without the power of the Creator who created them and who keeps them in existence, they would be nothing just as before the creation. They understand that there is nothing in the world but God. For this reason, explains Michel of Zlotchov, it is just the opposite of what most people think. When people are not attached to the divine no-thingness but to

earthly things, then they think they exist and, in their own eyes, are important and great. But how can someone be great when one night he exists and then dies in his sleep? Such a person's days are like a passing shadow and his life is all vanity. Thus if you think that you exist, then you don't. This is not the case, however, if you think that you are nothing because of your attachment to the Ayn Sof. Then you become like a drop which has fallen into the ocean. You have returned to your source, you are one with the waters of the sea, and it is no longer possible to recognize you as a separate being.

Where to Go from Here:

*L*isted here are six of my favorite "easy" introductions to Kabbalah for the reader who wishes to continue his or her study.

Buber, Martin, *Hasidism and Modern Man,* trans. and ed. Maurice Friedman. Humanities Press International, 1988. The best single book I know on the spiritual-mystical dimension of Judaism. Richly poetic. Probably best read aloud with a friend.

Heschel, Abraham J., "The Mystical Element in Judaism," in *The Jews: Their History, Culture, and Religion,* ed. Louis Finkelstein. Greenwood Press, Westport, Conn., Vol. II, 932-953. An elegant summary of Kabbalah by one of the great mystics of the 20th century.

Jacobs, Louis, *Jewish Mystical Testimonies*, Schocken, New York, 1977. An anthology of first-person mystical accounts from ancient times to the present with introductions and notes.

Kushner, Lawrence, *Honey from the Rock: Visions of Jewish Mystical Renewal*, Woodstock, Vt., Jewish Lights Publishing, 1995. A more accurate subtitle might have been "confessions of a suburban, liberal mystic."

Matt, Daniel C., *The Essential Kabbalah: The Heart of Jewish Mysticism*, Harper San Francisco, 1995. A concise sampling of primary Jewish mystical texts translated into easy English, with notes.

Scholem, Gershom G., *On the Kabbalah and its Symbolism*, trans. Ralph Manheim, Schocken, New York, 1965. Five in-depth essays by the master historian of Kabbalah scholarship.

*Books by
Lawrence Kushner*

The Book of Letters: A Mystical Alef-Bait,
Woodstock, Vt., Jewish Lights Publishing,
1990.

Honey from the Rock: Visions of Jewish
Mystical Renewal, Woodstock, Vt., Jewish
Lights Publishing, 1995.

The River of Light: Spirituality, Judaism,
Consciousness, Woodstock, Vt., Jewish Lights
Publishing, 1990.

God Was in This Place And I, I Did Not
Know: Finding Self, Spirituality and Ultimate
Meaning, Woodstock, Vt., Jewish Lights
Publishing, 1991.

The Book of Words: Talking Spiritual Life, Living Spiritual Talk, Woodstock, Vt., Jewish Lights Publishing, 1993.

The Book of Miracles: A Young Person's Guide to Jewish Spiritual Awareness, Special 10th Anniversary Edition, Woodstock, Vt., Jewish Lights Publishing, 1997.

The Invisible Chariot: An Introduction to Kabbalah and Spirituality for Young Adults, with Deborah Kerdeman, Denver, Colo., Alternatives in Religious Education, 1986.

Sparks Beneath the Surface: A Spiritual Commentary on the Torah, with Kerry M. Olitzky, Northvale, N.J., Jason Aronson, 1993.

Invisible Lines of Connection: Sacred Stories of the Ordinary, Woodstock, Vt., Jewish Lights Publishing, 1996. Also paperback.

Eyes Remade for Wonder: A Lawrence Kushner Reader, with an introduction by Thomas Moore, Woodstock, Vt., Jewish Lights Publishing, 1998.